Pebble® Plus

Animal Camouflage in the Desert

Hidden in Nature

by Martha E. H. Rustad

Consulting Editor: Gail Saunders-Smith, PhD
Consultant: Tanya Dewey, PhD
University of Michigan Museum of Zoology

Capstone press®

Mankato, Minnesota

Pebble Plus is published by Capstone Press,
151 Good Counsel Drive, P.O. Box 669, Mankato, Minnesota 56002.
www.capstonepress.com

 Books published by Capstone Press are manufactured with paper
containing at least 10 percent post-consumer waste.

Library of Congress Cataloging-in-Publication Data
Rustad, Martha E. H. (Martha Elizabeth Hillman), 1975–
    Animal camouflage in the desert / Martha E. H. Rustad.
    p. cm. — (Pebble Plus. Hidden in nature)
    Includes bibliographical references and index.
    Summary: "Simple text and photographs present animals that are camouflaged in the desert" — Provided
by publisher.
    ISBN 978-1-4296-3326-0 (library binding)
    1. Desert animals — Juvenile literature. 2. Camouflage (Biology) — Juvenile literature. I. Title. II. Series.
QL116.R87 2010
591.47'2 — dc22   2009007303

Editorial Credits
Erika L. Shores, editor; Abbey Fitzgerald, designer; Svetlana Zhurkin, media researcher

Photo Credits
Alamy/David South, 19; Don Mammoser, 17; SNAP/Daniel L. Geiger, 9; Steven J. Kazlowski, 11
Minden Pictures/Barry Mansell, 5
Nature Picture Library/Hanne & Jens Eriksen, 13
Peter Arnold/BIOS/Pierre Huguet, 15
Shutterstock/Casey K. Bishop, 1; Joshua Haviv, cover; Rusty Dodson, 21; SouWest Photography, 7

Note to Parents and Teachers

The Hidden in Nature set supports national science standards related to life science. This book
describes and illustrates animal camouflage in the desert. The images support early readers
in understanding the text. The repetition of words and phrases helps early readers learn new
words. This book also introduces early readers to subject-specific vocabulary words, which are
defined in the Glossary section. Early readers may need assistance to read some words and to
use the Table of Contents, Glossary, Read More, Internet Sites, and Index sections of the book.

Table of Contents

In the Desert

In a rocky, dry world,

it's good to blend in.

Camouflage helps animals

hide in the desert.

Kori bustards hide

in desert grass.

Brown and white feathers

help them blend in.

Bugs in the Desert

Grasshoppers in the desert

match rocks and sand.

They stay hidden

from predators.

Desert tarantulas look like
their surroundings.
They sneak up on grasshoppers
hiding in the desert.

Ground mantids hide
from predators and prey.
Mantids use their front legs
to grab insects.

Mammals in the Desert

A camel's shaggy brown fur
blends in with desert sand.
Long eyelashes keep sand
out of the camel's eyes.

Spots camouflage bobcats

in desert grass and bushes.

Bobcats sneak up

on rodents and rabbits.

Reptiles in the Desert

Spiky skin helps thorny devils look like prickly desert plants. These reptiles can also change color.

Black and brown markings hide
sidewinders in sand and rocks.
These snakes move through
sand sideways to find prey.

Glossary

bustard — a large heavy bird that runs more than it flies

camouflage — coloring or covering that makes animals look like their surroundings

insect — a small animal with a hard outer shell, six legs, three body sections, and two antennas; most insects have wings.

predator — an animal that hunts other animals for food

prey — an animal hunted by another animal for food

reptile — a cold-blooded animal that breathes air and has a backbone; most reptiles have scales.

rodent — a mammal with long front teeth used for gnawing

shaggy — long, rough hair

Read More

Mitchell, Susan K. *Animals with Crafty Camouflage: Hiding in Plain Sight*. Amazing Animal Defenses. Berkeley Heights, N.J.: Enslow, 2009.

Whitehouse, Patricia. *Hiding in a Desert*. Animal Camouflage. Chicago: Heinemann Library, 2003.

Internet Sites

FactHound offers a safe, fun way to find Internet sites related to this book. All of the sites on Facthound have been researched by our staff.

Here's all you do:

Visit *www.facthound.com*

FactHound will fetch the best sites for you!

Index

Word Count: 143

Grade: 1

Early-Intervention Level: 18